FIND YOUR HAPPY!

7 Steps to a More Fulfilling Life

Dr. Calvin E. Moore, Jr.

Happiness

Find Your Happy! 7 Steps to a More Fulfilling Life

Copyright © 2014 by Dr. Calvin E. Moore, Jr., Birmingham, Alabama

ISBN-13:
978-1494480028

ISBN-10:
1494480026

Dedication

For my mother Princess who deserves all the happiness she can find!

Table of Contents

Preface

An inalienable right, happiness is the meaning and the purpose of life, the whole aim and end of human existence.
--Aristotle

Like so many people, I have been on a personal quest for happiness for many years now. While my life has been wrought with pain, loss, and disappointment, I have also experienced love, joy, and contentment. Life does ebb and flow. For this reason we often experience what I call "fleeting happiness." While no one should expect to always be happy, I firmly believe happiness is a choice and we must pursue it. However, there are some ingredients needed in order for happiness to manifest itself in our lives. This book contains my notions about those essential elements. During the writing of this book I discovered a wonderful website (www.happycounts.org) that contains many of the things I believe we have to focus on during our pursuit of happiness. There I found the following graphic of some of the things that are essential to finding happiness in life. It is called the *Gross National Happiness Index*. It sounds complicated, but it represents the *domains of happiness* or the conditions by which we determine our overall balance and satisfaction with life. There is also a survey on the website that will generate your *"happiness index"* based on these domains. As I looked at the graphic along with my results I realized that for the first time I had some idea just how happy I was in a tangible way. I encourage you to take the survey too.

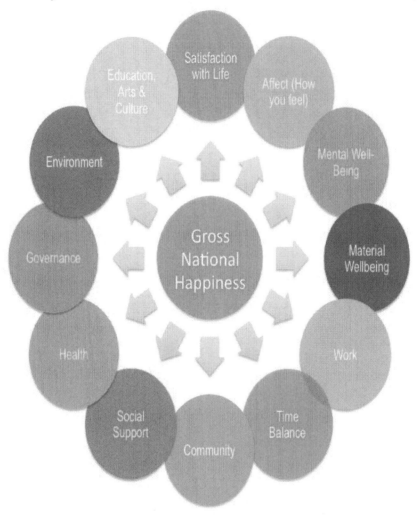

Source: www.happycounts.org

The *Gross National Happiness Index* is about well-being, not just being happy. I have realized that happiness is complex. It is not merely finding your soulmate or working a dream job. It is what I like to call "life's sweet spot" a place of complete contentment and agreement. The bible refers to this as *"an even place"* in Psalms 26:12. This is a divine habitation for us and it is worth the effort.

Each chapter is devoted to one of the seven steps toward finding happiness in your life. I decided during my research to begin each Chapter of this book with a famous quote related to the content. I hope these quotes will bring the text alive for the reader and illustrate how universal life's experiences are for each of us. You will also notice the use of Chinese symbols on the title page of the book. While living in Washington, DC I had a picture of the Chinese symbol for "Happiness" in my kitchen. It was a constant reminder of my quest for happiness. I think these symbols are elegant and beautiful. I wanted to share their beauty with the reader.

Some people may wonder why I am not writing about finding joy. Well that is a good question. Joy is the end result. I would propose to the reader that you can't end up with a joyful life without pursuing what makes you happy. This book is about the search for true happiness. There are seven essential steps toward living a more fulfilling life—knowing who you are; forgiveness; letting go of the past; shedding past hurts and disappointments; eliminating toxic relationships; loving God; and loving yourself. Following these simple steps will place you on a path toward happiness and ultimately a more joyful life. *Find Your Happy!*

Chapter One

Who are you?

Be yourself; everyone else is already taken.
— Oscar Wilde

Happiness is about our lives as a whole: it includes the fluctuating feelings we experience everyday but also our overall satisfaction with life. It is influenced by our genes, upbringing and our external circumstances - such as our health, our work and our financial situation. But crucially it is also heavily influenced by our choices - our inner attitudes, how we approach our relationships, our personal values and our sense of purpose (http://www.actionforhappiness.org/why-happiness). However, it begins with a deep understanding of who you are. This is the first step toward a more fulfilling life. You cannot be truly happy if you don't know who you are or if you are not comfortable in your own skin. The bible tells us that we were *fearfully and wonderfully made* in Psalms 139:14. We are made in God's image. How cool is that? This scripture demonstrates how unique and marvelous we are compared to the rest of creation. Each of us are unique as individuals as well and knowing that should give us a reason to appreciate who we are. I have never been uncomfortable with who I am. I think I was born with a level of confidence that some people simply don't have. I wish I could bottle it and sell it because I would become a millionaire. You are important and it is about time you act like it! Just remember that this attitude can make those around you a bit unsettled, but don't worry about that because being comfortable in your own skin is essential to being happy. Your happiness is our goal.

Society spends a lot to time, effort, and money telling us what to think, who to love, what to wear, and yes who we are. You cannot accept these definitions. There were seasons in my life when I felt like I was too black, too skinny, too poor, and even too educated. I have also felt as though I was not enough—not black enough, not from the right family, not polished enough, and yes, not even man enough. But none of those things were true. The truth is that I am enough, just the way I am. Of course everyone can be a better person, but that is not what I am talking about here. I had to realize that I have to define those things for myself.

In the summer of my senior year in high school I had decided to join the Army reserve. I thought it was a good idea at the time. Like all of the new recruits in Alabama I had to go to Maxwell Air Force Base in Montgomery, Alabama for the physical exam and intake processing. When I arrived they took my weight. I was one pound underweight for my height. The young man checking me in said, "You better try to eat something to gain one pound tonight because they won't take you if you are underweight." That evening I ate a huge meal and tried my best to gain one pound. The next morning I was still one pound underweight and they refused to take me in. Now I was devastated initially and spent a lot of time thinking about how unfair it was, but I couldn't do anything about the weight standards. I decided to register for college and four years later I had gained the pound I needed. I enlisted in the Air Force. There was nothing wrong with the military standards and there was nothing wrong with me. The truth is that my life was not yet in *agreement* with my choice. *Agreement* is a state of being in harmony or accord in your life. It is more than mere balance it is the place in our life when choice and purpose collide. I could have spent years feeling rejected by the military and depressed about being underweight. I didn't do any of that. Instead I enrolled in college and developed a plan to strategically gain the weight I needed to join the military. I accepted who I was at the time and set out to line my physical body up with what I wanted in my life. Mind, body and spirit have to be in harmony. Happiness is about finding agreement.

I also had to realize that in order to be fulfilled I had to start being the best me I could be. It no longer mattered what others thought about me. Steve Jobs once said, "Your time is limited, so don't waste it living someone else's life. Don't be trapped by dogma - which is living with the results of other people's thinking. Don't let the noise of other's opinions drown out your own inner voice. And most important have the courage to follow your heart and intuition. They somehow already know what you truly want to become. Everything else is secondary." He is suggesting that if we look deep enough and listen close enough we already know who we are. But we often let others talk us out of it. I am not doing that anymore. I am going to always listen to my own inner voice.

There are four things you can do to discover who you are. They are sequential and build upon each other so complete them in order.

1. **Create a family tree.** This activity seems too simple right? You'd be surprised how many people have never really done this. You can't know who you are without doing a family tree. This can be done even if you don't know your biological family. That is not the sole purpose of this activity. In many ways we define who our family is and what they mean to us. You cannot understand who you are without connecting to where you came from—even when that place is not perfect. Writing it down makes it tangible for you and gives you insight. I have included a "My Family Tree" graphic on page 46 to help you with this important activity. On the bottom of that page write down three major life goals for yourself. It doesn't matter if you have achieved them or not. Writing them here with your family tree is essential because they should line up with where you came from. I believe our life goals are in our DNA. They reflect who we are.

2. **Write down your core values and beliefs.** We are all driven by a set of core values and beliefs. Many times these are established by others in our lives or outside influences. This is your opportunity to create your own life principles with your own voice. By writing them down you are affirming your commitment to these values and beliefs going forward. This helps create *agreement* in your life. These core beliefs define you. They are who you are in a fundamental way. Without them you are not distinct or inimitable.

3. **Trust yourself.** Now that you have created your family tree with your life goals and written down your values and beliefs you can begin what I believe is your most difficult task during

this process—trust yourself. Remember what I said at the onset, happiness is about our lives as a whole—the good and the bad; love and hurt; and triumphs and defeats. All those experiences make us who we are today. Don't be afraid to trust yourself with who you have become.

4. **Practice what you preach.** I don't think I need to elaborate on this one. Now that you have defined who you are for yourself—be.

You have completed your first step to finding your Happy!

Source: http://www.actionforhappiness.org

Reflection Activity

Reflecting on Chapter 1 begin a journal and describe new learning, understandings, and contradictions about who you are and what your purpose is in life. Complete your family tree on page 46. This is the first step to living a more fulfilling life.

Chapter Two

Forgive

The weak can never forgive. Forgiveness is the attribute of the strong.
--Mahatma Gandhi

Ernest Hemingway told a story of a father and his teenage son who had a relationship that had become strained to the point of breaking. Finally the son ran away from home. His father, however, began a journey in search of his rebellious son. Finally, in Madrid, in a last desperate effort to find him, the father put an ad in the newspaper. The ad read: "DEAR PACO, MEET ME IN FRONT OF THE NEWSPAPER OFFICE AT NOON. ALL IS FORGIVEN. I LOVE YOU. --YOUR FATHER." The next day at noon in front of the newspaper office, 800 "Pacos" showed up. The second step to happiness is *Forgiveness*, which is defined as a conscious, deliberate decision to release feelings of resentment or vengeance toward a person or group who has harmed you, regardless of whether they actually deserve your forgiveness (http://greatergood.berkeley.edu). Forgiveness is a megatheme in the bible. But I agree with Gandhi only the strong can forgive.

I want to begin this discourse with my own journey in trying to walk in forgiveness, which can be very difficult. I am a giver by nature. It is just part of the fabric of who I am. The interesting part is that I somehow always ended up in relationships with takers. Now this is an accident waiting to happen. Just to be clear I am talking about any relationship not just romantic relationships. Takers come in all shapes and sizes. Givers attract takers. In my life I had family members, lovers, and friends who were takers. I

14

feel obligated to say to my family members and friends reading this that I am not talking about them, at least not specifically. I am speaking generally. I have wonderful and important family and friends whom I treasure. Nor do I want to give takers a bad name here—it is just their nature. I have matured and learned they don't mean to cause heartache and some of the people in your life who are takers honestly may not even characterize themselves that way. Nonetheless for many years I was hurt and abused by many of the takers in my life. They just drained me dry. At first I didn't notice because it gave me pleasure to give. I noticed after I became bitter and gripped by not forgiving them. I had to let go of the feelings of disappointment and regret.

What I regretted the most was not asking for what I wanted and needed in the relationship and blaming them when I didn't get it. In fact it was my fault for not doing that and it was unfair to be angry with them for not reading my mind. I had to forgive. I remember this one friend who I always gave 100 percent to in the relationship while only receiving 25 percent in return—honestly. I became bitter and really lashed out at them for their indifference without explaining what I needed from them. I ended the friendship without forgiving them. Years later I learned they had moved on to another giver and repeated the cycle, which is what most takers do. I not only forgave the person, but I explained what I had learned in an effort to help them mature and be more of a true friend in their life.

There is a lesson here for the giver and the taker in a relationship. The giver has to work at asking for what they need and holding the taker accountable. Likewise the taker has to be conscious and responsive. Because it is not in their nature to give they have to work at it intentionally. Believe it or not this arrangement can be perfect if both people are mature and aware of the role they play.

I have often said because we are human we have challenges with forgiveness. We can forgive, but we don't forget. I actually don't believe forgetting should be our focus. The focus is to genuinely forgive those who have done you harm and make sure your behavior is in agreement with the act of forgiveness. If you have truly forgiven someone your behavior will line up. In other words, you will "act" as if you have forgotten what they did to you. Well you might ask how this is possible. It takes discipline and a lot of effort.

There is another challenge. We should walk in forgiveness. We have to be quick to forgive others when they have wronged us. I used to let things fester and build up. That was a terrible way to live and it weighed me down. You can't be happy with a lot of un-forgiveness in your heart and soul. There are three things that I do in order to walk in forgiveness and be ready to forgive when necessary:

1. **Learn to give and receive.** As I said earlier people can be divided into two categories—givers and takers. In order to find fulfillment in life you have to position yourself to give and receive. Regardless of what is most comfortable for you (giving or taking) remember to ask for what you want in a relationship and remember to be responsive too.

16

2. **Communicate.** The key to any endeavor is communication. No one can read your mind except God. Be mindful of both what you are communicating and how you are communicating. I have learned that I get into more trouble when I use the wrong tone to convey a message. Communication is an art. It includes listening—active listening. Don't get so caught up in delivering your message that you forget to listen.

3. **Let it go!** Forget about the hurt. You have to let go and learn the lesson. This is easier said than done. But remember focusing on the hurt blinds us from the lesson. Regardless of how deep the wounds of a bad relationship are there is a lesson to be learned. Let it go and learn.

Relationships are complex and tricky to manage. They are also seasonal. People come and go in your life. If you are going to walk in forgiveness and be happy you have to learn to identify the purpose of the people you let into your life. It is likely they will hurt you, but the purpose might help you deal with it and move on. As I was writing this chapter I began to reflect on the people in my life that I hurt deeply. I quickly realized that you can only hurt those who love you. This was a profound revelation. I was so disappointed in myself and immediately reached out to the people I had hurt and asked them to forgive me. Yes walking in forgiveness means living without offense. I hope you do the same in your quest for happiness. In doing so you will have accomplished step two in your journey—forgive!

Reflection Activity

Reflecting on Chapter 2 continue your journal entries by documenting a time when you were forgiven. Also consider this scripture – 1 Corinthians **13:4-7** _Love is patient and kind; love does not envy or boast; it is not arrogant or rude. It does not insist on its own way; it is not irritable or resentful; it does not rejoice at wrongdoing, but rejoices with the truth. Love bears all things, believes all things, hopes all things, endures all things._ Describe how this scripture relates to forgiving others and you benefited from such an act of kindness.

Chapter Three

Let Go of the Past

If you let it go, you can have it all
--author unknown

Two monks were on a pilgrimage. One day, they came to a deep river. At the edge of the river, a young woman sat weeping because she was afraid to cross the river without help. She begged the two monks to help her. The younger monk turned his back. The members of their order were forbidden to touch a woman.

But the older monk picked up the woman without a word and carried her across the river. He put her down on the far side and continued his journey. The younger monk came after him, scolding him and berating him for breaking his vows. He went on this way for a long time. Finally, at the end of the day the older monk turned to the younger one and said, "I only carried her across the river. You have been carrying her all day."

Like forgiveness, letting go can be tough. Usually there are a lot of things we need to let go of—people, ideas, expectations, desires, bad habits, false beliefs and unhealthy relationships. Why is letting go of these things so challenging? I think it is because of the emotion often associated with these things, especially people. Cat O'Connor suggests, "Every day, every moment presents an opportunity to create ourselves anew, to shrug off the baggage of the past, open ourselves up to the possibility of the moment and take action to create an incredible future." Isn't that unbelievably encouraging? I want to live in that space--the space of renewal. O'Connor reminds me of a passage in the bible that refers to "new mercies" that are available to us every morning. Wow! Lamentations 3:23 reads, *Great is His faithfulness. His mercies are new every morning.* What a concept? I get to start anew each day. I can let go of the baggage of yesterday daily.

Think for a moment about all the pain, hurt, disappointments, and frustrations of the past. If you are going to spend your time thinking about anything in your past, think of the good things—not the things that bring you pain. Let it go! This is an easy concept to understand, but difficult to actualize. So it takes practice. The only way you can truly be happy in your life is to shed the trappings of the past and look forward to a dynamic and promising future.

I remember many years ago when I was in a serious relationship with a school age sweetheart. I started liking this girl in the fourth grade. Oddly enough it was a long distance relationship because she lived in Detroit, Michigan and I was living in Birmingham, Alabama. Her grandmother lived right next door to my family and she would visit every summer. She was the first girl I held hands with, kissed, etc. As we got older the relationship became more serious. We planned to spend the rest of our lives together. When the relationship ended I was devastated. I went into a deep depression. I simply couldn't let it go. I was in the Air Force at the time and went on with my life. I went to work every day, but I wasn't alive anymore. I was dead inside. The pain and the hurt of this broken relationship was hard enough, but not being willing to let it go was killing me. It took me four years to get over that relationship and let it go. Because of the lost momentum it took me another ten years to trust someone else. That was a total of fourteen years wasted dwelling in the past. No one can afford to waste that much time. I don't want that for you. Learn from my mistake and let go now.

I had to train my mind over again. Because God created us with memory it is hard to let go of the hurt and pain of past experiences. Those experiences seep into our consciousness and began to affect every aspect of our lives. You have to begin turning those negatives into positives. One way to train your mind to do this is to practice positive self-talk. Self-talk or inner speech is one of the things that separate us from other species. Lev Vygotsky actually suggested this skill is closely associated with cognition. The truth is that we are always talking to ourselves. Our actions are determined by our thoughts. Everything begins in the mind. Letting go of the past includes changing the narrative, so we must actively re-train our mind with a new story. This self-talk must be positive and self-affirming. Here are some examples:

- I am moving forward
- I can take care of this
- I am trying
- I am in control of this
- I am talented
- I know my potential
- I will succeed

Joel Osteen calls them "I AM" statements. I have started using them to help me let go of the past and create a new future.

- I am powerful
- I am intelligent
- I am well and whole
- I am a problem solver
- I am creative
- I am beautiful
- I am enough

You should make your own list of I AM statements and declare them every day. Change the narrative in your life and let go of the past. O'Connor has some action steps that should help us let go of our past and jumpstart our future

    1. Meditate. Find stillness, breathe. Meditation is action. Our mind is much harder to still than our body. Our lives are busy and fast paced, filled with external noise and distractions. Clarity comes from quiet. Meditation, even in small amounts, will make room for the next 9 steps.

    2. Understand. Take time to reflect on your own history as a third party looking in without judgment: simply observe. Understand that you are not your past. Understand that the situations and patterns and people in your life created your experiences, they didn't create you. Knowing and understanding your past and some of your patterns will help you to recognize why you hold on and repeat self-destructive behaviors. Understanding creates awareness; awareness helps you break the cycle.

    3. Accept. Accept your history and the people that have been a part of your history; accept your circumstances and remember that none of these define you. Acceptance is the first step to letting go and setting yourself free. Learn from the monk in the story: carrying bitterness, anger or animosity burdens no one but you.

4. Empty your cup. Consciously and actively work at letting go of your story; your judgments and ideals, the material things, all your stuff. They have no real value. They do not make you stronger, healthier or more powerful, and belief in them is a delusion. Pour out your expectations of how, who, where and what you should be as they, too, are part of a story that holds you back from simply being. Once you let go of this story and empty your cup, your life purpose will open up and flow.

5. Align. Take a moment (or several: you're worth the time) to write down the following:

i. Your core beliefs/values

ii. Your Life Goals

iii. The actions that you are taking to pursue those goals.

Now take an honest look at your core beliefs/values and determine whether or not they align with your goals and actions. If not, ask yourself: is it time to create new core beliefs, set new goals OR take new action? What actions must you take to align your actions with your beliefs in order to attain your goals. Write down 3 actions that you will take this week to get yourself moving.

6. Flex. It may seem paradoxical to detach from outcomes, yet set goals and work toward them. But if you are flexible -- that is, willing to let go of the end result -- aligning your goals and true purpose with the greater good is righteous action. Be flexible; allow the path to unfold as it will, opening up to opportunities. Flex and flow with the current of life.

7. Contribute. When you find yourself lamenting about your past or angry about your present or brooding about your future, find a way to making someone's day better. Offering a smile to someone as you pass, opening a door, putting a bit of extra change in the parking meter, dropping off some food for the food bank: these simple actions can have lasting impact and help you to put your situation into perspective. Contributing to the well-being of others is the best way to align with your true self.

8. Believe in yourself. Believe in your purpose. Believe that the universe is unfolding as it should and that you have a divine roll to play. Believe that holding on does nothing in fact but hold you back from that purpose.

9. Love the process. Have fun. Be playful, cheerful and positive. Give power to positivity. Love yourself, love others and love this life. It is a gift to unwrap each and every day, to gaze upon with new and excited eyes.

10. Be grateful. Be true. Once you have taken all of these actions, just be.

Finally, the quote at the beginning of this chapter was first told to me by one of my best friends—Patrice Dawson. She said to me one day when I was feeling down, "If you let it go, you can have it all!" She was right. You have to let go in order to make room for

24

something new. Letting go of someone doesn't mean you don't care about them. It just means that you care about yourself more. Remember you are the only person you can control. So don't be afraid to let them go. Be happy! They always come back anyway.

Source:
http://www.mindbodygreen.com/0-4116/10-Tips-to-Let-Go-of-the-Past-Embrace-the-Future.html

Reflection Activity

Reflecting on Chapter 3 continue your journal entries by writing your own "I AM" statements. Recite them every morning for the next 30 days. Document in journal the difference these statements have made in your life.

Chapter Four

They Always Come Back!

Relationships are like glass. Sometimes it's better to leave them broken than try to hurt yourself putting it back together.

-- Author Unknown

Relationships are usually a main source of happiness, but they can also bring heartache and distress. I remember talking about this with one of my closest friends. She had been in a relationship for a couple of years and was head-over-heels in love with this guy. As a good friend I stood by her side during all the struggle and pain of the relationship that had long stopped benefitting her. She had come to the point where she wanted to end it and to my amazement she did. I knew it was hard because she loved him. My reply to her was, "They always come back!" She seems surprised by my statement at first, but a few months later I received a call from her. She was so excited. She had gotten a call from an ex-boyfriend. She had not heard from him in several years. He had come back. I immediately explained that ninety percent of the time he will come back—especially if you are a good woman. The only reason a man doesn't come back to a good woman is that he can't.

The story is common. A couple meets, dates and began to connect and for whatever reason go months without speaking. Then he or she calls you! Eventually my friend also received one of these calls from the guy she was in love with. This may seem like good news, but it could be the beginning of a pattern. Some men recognize a good woman and may come back with good intentions. Others may just be lonely and looking for a one-night-stand so women you need to be prepared for both scenarios. While I can only really speak from a man's perspective, I believe a woman knows a good man too. Don't be confused. This actually applies to both genders. One thing to remember is that it is your decision when he or she comes back. They may not be coming back talking about regret or telling you how sorry they are for leaving. Sometimes they think coming back should speak for itself. Don't be fooled by any of that. You have to decide if you want them back. Remember finding your "life's sweet spot" is at stake. That is what you should focus on when you get that call.

Be careful with this because it will be emotional, especially if you were in love. So it doesn't matter if it is a text message saying "hi" or a knock at the door, or a phone call—they always come back. In order to help you deal with this situation I have some helpful tips:

1. **Stay Calm.** There is no reason to get excited yet. After all they could just be saying "hi" and a simple reply is all that is required. Try not to read too much into it. This is more important if it has been a long time since there has been contact. Men, in particular are prone to reaching out if they are bored or lonely. Men are natural predators and we tend to go on the prowl when relationships end. Women are a little different. When they come back its more about regret and truly missing the relationship or its benefits. Stay calm and enjoy the moment.

2. **Start Planning**. The end of a relationship is a good time to reflect and re-think what you really want in your life. Start planning your next move. It is not the time to dive into another relationship—especially the one you just left. While there is nothing wrong with giving someone another chance, make sure it fits with this plan you are developing. Be clear and up front. Maybe being friends is your destiny because not every relationship is meant to last. Consider that it will take more than a random phone call or text message to rekindle a relationship.

3. **It's Your Decision.** It took me a long time to realize that relationships are seasonal. Not everyone will be part of your life forever. There are also many reasons why relationships fail. So if you and your ex have both grown during the separation this may be a good time to discuss what you need now—not relive the past. Whatever you decide it's yours. Don't let others make the decision for you. I am sure your family and friends all have an opinion. You decide. Do what makes you happy. This is about the pursuit of happiness, not the one that got away. Many times relationships stop serving or benefiting us. Women tend to have a more difficult time letting go because of the uncertainty of starting over. Men are different. Men are more concerned about convenience and comfort. Decide what you need to be happy and pursue it with reckless abandonment.

Don't get hung up on the reasons why someone left or why they are coming back. Don't bring up whose fault it was. Try to start over. Focus instead on where you are in your life. More importantly ask for what you want. If you take them back own that decision and remember they already left you once so don't be surprised if it doesn't work out. While I do recommend keeping expectations low, hold them accountable. It might actually work out this time. When relationships end both parties are at fault. You participated too. In chapter two I talked a lot about givers and takers. Apply what you learned to this situation and do something different. What you did last time didn't work, right?

Finally, I remember many years ago when I was dealing with a break-up and considering taking back an ex. My best friend at the time told me not to do it. They said, "There are too many fish in the sea!" At the time I wondered what sea they were fishing in. Now I have come to understand when you catch a fish it's hard to through it back into the sea. The end of a relationship is hard, but you can get over it. Realizing that it is very likely your ex will show up again is important. Stay calm. Stick to your plan. Make a decision. Be happy!

Reflection Activity

Reflecting on Chapter 4 continue with your journal writing by making a list of past relationships where you might not have gotten the closure you needed. What could you do to bring closure to those relationships and move forward?

Chapter Five

They Hurt You, So What!

The truth is everyone is going to hurt you. You just got to find the ones worth suffering for. — Bob Marley

I thought being hurt was the story of my life. While writing this book I realized it's the story of everyone's life. We have all been hurt. I can't express how freeing it was for me when I realized I was not alone in my circumstances. As I said earlier, we were fearfully and wonderfully made. Unfortunately, that includes being deeply emotional creatures. That is one of the reasons being hurt is so common. I personally believe you can only be hurt by those who love you. I know this seems strange and I may be the only person who will tell you this fact. Imagine yourself in the center of a large circle. When you love someone and the feelings are mutual, you allow them inside the circle. You let them in because you value them greatly and feel valued by them. You grant them access. People with this kind of access have certain privileges and permissions. Yes, you give them permission or power to hurt you. Of course hurting you is an abuse of the power you give them, but trust me it happens. They have access and it's the access that gives them permission. The people outside your circle seldom have such access and when they do it is usually by accident. The kind of offenses perpetrated by these associates is not as impactful. You are not hurt by them because they are not as valued as someone you love.

I began this chapter with a quote from Bob Marley. I chose it because it's provocative. I never thought of Bob Marley as a philosopher. I grew up with an appreciation for his music and the lyrics, but when I read this quote I began to study his life. What I found was a man with a kind of folk wisdom. He was worth listening to when he spoke. Many of his interviews were fascinating. He was pensive and meditative—and even brooding at times. I have thought a lot about the meaning of his quote and whether it's true or not. I have come to the conclusion that I agree with his truth. He is simply saying loving someone outweighs the risk of being hurt by them. When you love someone you don't mind suffering for them even when they hurt you. If you must suffer you must also search for the ones worth the pain and hurt they will inevitably cause you in the long run.

Now I am not making excuses for the hurt you will experience. Nor am I talking about the minor infractions we deal with in life (i.e., someone hurting your feelings or being rude, etc.). I am speaking of major offenses that damage us in some way. When a loved one hurts us deeply it causes us distress and humiliation. We are often so unhappy that we are paralyzed. I am hoping to frame this discourse in a way that brings about an understanding because the hurt is more devastating when a person who loves you does it.

It's also important that we acknowledge what we are feeling when we are hurt—the anger, injustice, and hatred—and recognize how hurt we are. At the same time we must avoid suppressing our feelings because they fester. Let it all out in some way—exercise, write in your journal, take up a hobby. Don't let the hurt run your life because negative feelings can zap our energy, especially when we hold on to them and they create an emotional bond with the abuser that keeps the feelings alive so that we keep replaying the drama and conflict over in our heads, justifying our own behavior and disregarding theirs. In the process we become a not-very-happy person.

So I say to you, they hurt you so what! Turn it all around using these simple techniques by Ed and Deb Shapiro:

1. Recognize no one harms another unless they are in pain themselves. Ever noticed how, when you're in a good mood, it's hard for you to harm or hurt anything? You may even take the time to get an insect out of the sink. But if you're stressed or in a bad mood, then how easy it is to wash it down the drain.

2. No one can hurt you unless you let them. Hard to believe, as no one actually wants to be hurt but it's true. When someone hurts us, we are inadvertently letting them have an emotional hold over us.

3. Respect yourself enough that you want to feel good. You have to make the decision that you won't respond to the negativity despite what others do. This puts you in control of the situation.

4. Consider how you may have contributed to the situation. It's all too easy to point fingers and blame the perpetrator but no difficulty is entirely one-sided. So contemplate your piece in the dialogue or what you may have done to add fuel to the fire. Even when they feels they are 100 percent right

5. Extend kindness. That doesn't mean you're like a doormat that lets others trample all over you while you just lie there and take it. But it does mean letting go of negativity sooner than you might have done before, so that you can replace it with compassion. Like an oyster that may not like that irritating grain of sand in its shell but manages to transform the irritation into a beautiful and precious pearl.

6. Meditate. Meditation takes the heat out of things and helps you cool off, so you don't over react. A daily practice we use is where we focus on a person we may be having difficulty with or is having a difficulty with us. We hold them in our hearts and say: May you be well! May you be happy! May all things go well for you!

Being hurt is not easy to deal with, but now you have the tools to turn the tables. Put your inner circle on notice. They don't have permission to hurt you anymore. In fact no one does. Remember your happiness is on the line here. You don't have time to waste being sidetracked by hurt. Teach the members of your inner circle these steps so that you all are playing by the same rules. The people you love should make your life better not worse. Love God. He will never hurt you!

Source:
http://www.care2.com/greenliving/what-you-can-do-when-someone-hurts-you.html

Reflection Activity

Reflecting on Chapter 5 continue your journal writing and describe new learning, understandings, and contradictions about meditation. Try sitting in silence in the morning before your day starts. Do this for a week and record your experience.

Chapter Six

Love God

Only God can fully satisfy the hungry heart of man.
- Hugh Black

Love is a universal truth. It doesn't matter what culture or ethnic group you belong to or the language you speak. Love is a concept that everyone understands. You can even see it being instinctively exhibited in other species. All of creation understands and displays love in some way. Love is also challenging. We experience love on many levels and in different forms. I like the different ways love is defined in the Ancient Greek language. These variations are used throughout the Bible as well.

Agape (ἀγάπη *agápē*) God's love. It generally refers to a "pure," ideal type of love, rather than the physical attraction suggested by *eros*. It has also been translated as "love of the soul."

Eros (ἔρως *érōs*) (from the Greek deity Eros) is passionate love, with sensual desire and longing. The Greek word *erota* means *in love*. Although eros is initially felt for a person, with contemplation it becomes an appreciation of the beauty within that person, or even becomes appreciation of beauty itself. Eros helps the soul recall knowledge of beauty and contributes to an understanding of spiritual truth. Lovers and philosophers are all inspired to seek truth by eros. Some translations list it as "love of the body."

Philia (φιλία _philía_), a dispassionate virtuous love. It includes loyalty to friends, family, and community, and requires virtue, equality, and familiarity. Philia is motivated by practical reasons; one or both of the parties benefit from the relationship. It can also mean "love of the mind."

Storge (στοργή _storgē_) is natural affection, like that felt by parents for offspring.

Xenia (ξενία _xenía_), hospitality, was an extremely important practice in Ancient Greece. It was an almost ritualized friendship formed between a host and his guest, who could previously have been strangers.

Source: http://en.wikipedia.org/wiki/Love

Because love is so deeply felt we experience joy and pain as a result. While most people who know me would say I am a romantic, I am also a realist. It is better to have experienced deep love, but it comes mostly with risk and great sacrifice. The only love without personal risk and sacrifice is our love for God. This is the supreme commandment for humankind. _You shall love the_ Lord _your God with all your heart and with all your soul and with all your might_ Deuteronomy 6:5. I have heard this all my life and understand the meaning, but have never really been taught "how" to do it. This practical teaching is important because loving God is the essential to finding happiness.

Loving with All Our Heart

While surprising to some, the old covenant recognized that a spiritual relationship with God begins from within, with a proper disposition toward the preeminent savior, sovereign, and satisfier. From the heart *"flow the springs of life"* (Proverbs 4:23), and without one's will, desires, passions, affections, perceptions, and thoughts rightly aligned, the life of love is impossible. In order to love God with all our heart He has to be the center of our lives. We can't be passionate about someone we don't know and love so we have to diligently seek His ways. He has shown how much He loves us by giving His only son for us. That is the reason I love Him and why I serve Him with such intensity.

Loving with All Our Soul

Along with our hearts, we are called to love God with all our soul. In the first five books of the Old Testament the "soul" refers to one's whole being as a living person, which includes one's "heart" but is so much more. For example, in Genesis 2:7 we are told that God formed the man of dust from the ground and breathed into his nostrils the breath of life, and the man became a living *soul"* I believe this refers to our entire being—the core of who we are—everything we are and what we do should reflect that we love God.

Loving with All Our Might

When I think of "might" I automatically think of power source, strength, or energy. The "strength" of a person can be articulated in many ways—money, influence, access, talent, physique, etc. Our love for God should be reflected in our strength and power. This actually encompasses everything we have available to us. We should honor God with those things.

One of my favorite songs is *Jesus You are the Center of My Joy!* God has to be the center of our joy. Without Him our quest for happiness is really in vain. It is through our love for Him that we find pleasure, hope, strength, and comfort. I don't think I could have made it through all of the difficult moments in my life without the constancy of God's love for me. He has been a faithful friend, a constant companion, and a present help! I have lived long enough to know why David danced out of his clothes in celebration of God's goodness and mercy. You can't experience God's love and not show gratitude. Hugh Black was onto something when he indicated that only God can satisfy us. I tried everything in my lifetime—drugs, sex, money, and ambition. I can truly say that I agree with his quote at the beginning of this chapter. Our desire and motives are insatiable—only God can fulfill us. It is when He becomes our desire that we become content, settled, and yes happy!

Reflection Activity

Reflecting on Chapter 6 continue your journal writing by describe new learning and understandings about loving God. How important is loving God in your quest for happiness?

Chapter Seven

Love Yourself

Believing in our hearts that who we are is enough is the key to a more satisfying and balanced life.

--Ellen Sue Stern

Loving yourself is the key to true happiness. Often times we don't even respect ourselves. I say this because if we loved and respected ourselves many of the things we go through would be dead on arrival. I chose this step as the final step for a reason, but it could have easily been the first step in our journey. Self-love is at the heart of joy and fulfillment in life. You can't love others if you don't love God and yourself. We have to love our life and the journey. It is the only life we get. Don't spend your time living with self-doubt and self-loathing. It's not a crime to love you. If you don't love you then don't expect anyone else to. Some people might think it is arrogant or being self-centered. Don't listen to them. Arielle Consoli says,

We spend so much time waiting to be loved, hoping love will find us, searching, and yearning for that special love. Feeling empty and lost without it. Wanting someone to give us love and fill us up. Unfortunately, that's not usually how life works. Loving yourself is mainly having self-respect, which is the only dependable way to create love in your own life to share with others. When you expect love from an external source, and someone or something does not fulfill your void and fantasies, then you will feel worse than before. To be able

41

to be loved, you must love and respect yourself as much as you do others. Understanding the effects of loving yourself will only enhance your ability to love others. By doing so, you are enabling positive energy and allowing for great situations to occur in your life. This guide will help. Never think that you're living your life for nothing. Every day, there are people coming in and out of the world, so spend it wisely and respect yourself. Sometimes we feel as if our lives rely on that one person. We think 'If I do this, he/she will like me.' We tend to waste time avoiding those certain people, and regret it later. We miss them, yearn for their love, and even waste birthday wishes on them. In order to love someone, you must love yourself.

Source: http://www.wikihow.com/Love-Yourself

I have learned the only persons I can truly depend on is God and me. I have also learned that I spend an awful amount of time with myself so I may as well enjoy it. I learned to like me and appreciate who I am. We all have to "learn" to love ourselves. After making God the center of your joy the next step is loving yourself fiercely. Like everything else in this book you have to do this with intention. Try these simple steps:

- **Treat Yourself.** My mother taught me this first tip. When I was young I noticed that when my mother got paid she rewarded herself first. Even though we had plenty of bill to pay she took the time to give herself a treat. The size of the treat didn't matter. It is a small kind of accomplishment to reward yourself when there are other priorities, but commit yourself to it and have fun. You deserve it!

- **Put Your Feelings First for a Change.** If you are like me you are always putting others first. The concept is nice, but it means that you never put yourself first. Then one day I wondered if anyone was putting me first. It's time to find your own voice and express your thoughts and aspirations. It is also okay to say no sometimes. I had a problem with saying no. Because I was the oldest son I ended up with a big brother syndrome. I didn't even realize it until one day a friend of mine blurted it out. She said, "You are always taking care of people. When are you going to start taking care of yourself?" I had put my feelings first for a change and that meant saying no.

- **Loving You is Attractive.** You should love yourself if no one else does. Loving who you are is powerful. It allows you to present yourself to the world with confidence. Confidence draws people. Others can tell you are comfortable in your own skin and respond to it. It's attractive!

I want to close this chapter with a true story. Many years ago a women fell in love with someone and after several years the person became indifferent. She could see all the signs, but didn't want to believe he didn't love her anymore. She tried everything she could to change the relationship. She even knew the relationship was not good for her, but she kept trying. Even though she wasn't happy she kept trying. Finally she discovered he had moved on without bothering to tell her. She was devastated. She even lashed out trying to get revenge. After two years of hurting and misery she began to slowly let go. She asked me to help her deal with the loss. During that time I made a discovery. I was dealing with some similar issues. In fact most of us are dealing with the distress of an unfulfilling relationship— whether it's a family member, friend, or lover. We are disrespecting ourselves by begging someone else to stay with us. I decided I wouldn't do it anymore. I began to say to myself I am good enough. She did too. Now she is on her way to a happy ending.

It took me a while longer. After helping her through her situation I started working on me. I followed the steps I shared in this book. I re-discovered who I was. I forgave those who hurt me. I let go of the past. I didn't let them come back. I got over the hurt. I love God. I love myself. I did the work and I have found agreement in my life. I am reclaiming life's sweet spot. I am happy!

Reflection Activity

Reflecting on Chapter 7 continue your journal writing by describing the love you have for yourself. The goal of this chapter is to love you fiercely. The Bible commands us to love our neighbors in the same manner that we love ourselves.

Appendices

My Family Tree

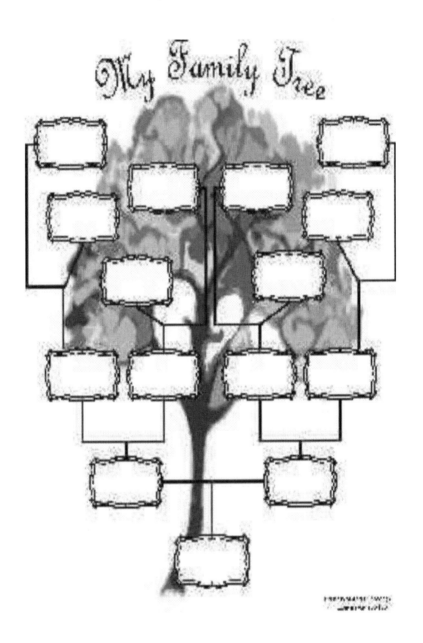

A Prayer for Happiness

Dear God give me the strength to follow you and realize your great love for me. Help me cope with the hurt and the pain that I may experience, Teach me to forgive others because you have forgiven me. Grant me the courage to be happy with you always in this life and the next. Amen

Self-Renewal Plan

Everyone needs some down time and a period when they disconnect from all the busyness in our lives. I believe this is so critical that we should plan it. There are so many things competing for our attention—family, church, career, community, and friends. Our lives are also inundated with technology. Everyone is tuned in to Twitter and Facebook—not to mention the many digital devices that keep us connected all the time. We all need a break!

I found this wonderful plan developed by Jan Marie Dore. Ms. Dore suggests, we all need to take ourselves away to be quiet, think and relax. She encourages a regular planned vacation so that we can return feeling renewed and rejuvenated in our lives. Following the following renewal tips will keep you recharged for life:

Passion is part of the self-renewed life, so try regularly to engage in activities you're passionate about to feel rejuvenated and inspired. Focus on your self-care, and let go of the guilt of getting your own needs met before others, as it is only by caring for yourself that you have the energy to care for others and to do your best work.

Take the time you need to rejuvenate, to clear your head and get off the treadmill of busyness - for this is the only life you'll have. Make self-renewal and constructive rest an integral part of your schedule by incorporating these ideas into your regular routine:

- Plan a quiet morning routine to set an intention and mood for the day;
- Leave your work at the office at the end of each day and week;
- Give yourself a break from the constant stress of responding to others by scheduling a personal retreat - time to be quiet, to think and relax, without the constant interference of TV, telephone and the Internet;
- Perform a routine activity more slowly and mindfully to experience the joy of the present moment;
- Plan fun, creative, or energizing things to do at least one day on the weekend; make it a priority to connect with other people to share a meal or an activity;
- Re-energize your spirit by regularly engaging in activities you're passionate about;
- Schedule blocks of time for regular renewal – a vacation, a retreat, an adventure—each week: a morning or afternoon, a day, a weekend.

Source: http://www.zeromillion.com/personaldev/self-renewal.html

Recommended Readings

1. The Compassionate Mind. Paul Gilbert
2. Emotional Intelligence. Daniel Goleman
3. The Happiness Hypothesis. Jonathan Haidt
4. Well-being: the Foundation of Hedonic Psychology. Edited by Daniel Kahneman, Ed Diener and Norbert Schwarz
5. Happiness: Lessons from a new Science. Richard Layard
6. The How of Happiness: A practical guide to getting the life you want. Sonja Lyubomirsky
7. Happiness: A guide to developing life's most important skill. Matthieu Ricard
8. The Expanding Circle. Peter Singer
9. The Science of Wellbeing. Edited by Felicia Huppert, Nick Baylis and Barry Keverne
10. Flourish: A New Understanding of Happiness and Well-Being - and How To Achieve Them. Martin Seligman

Source:http://www.actionforhappiness.org/why-happiness

Made in the USA
Columbia, SC
05 July 2022

62818431R00028